P9-EEJ-532

Bankston, John, 1974–
Jacques-Yves Cousteau :
his story under the sea /
[2003]
33305203763119
CU   02/26/03

Jacques-Yves Cousteau: His Story Under the Sea

John Bankston

Mitchell Lane
PUBLISHERS

SANTA CLARA COUNTY LIBRARY

3 3305 20376 3119

Unlocking the Secrets of Science

Profiling 20th Century Achievers in Science, Medicine, and Technology

Jacques-Yves Cousteau: His Story Under the Sea

Copyright © 2003 by Mitchell Lane Publishers, Inc. All rights reserved. No part of this book may be reproduced without written permission from the publisher. Printed and bound in the United States of America.

First Printing

Library of Congress Cataloging-in-Publication Data
Bankston, John, 1974-
    Jacques-Yves Cousteau: his story under the sea/John Bankston.
        p. cm. —(Unlocking the secrets of science)
    Includes bibliographical references (p.)
    Summary: Examines the life and accomplishments of the French oceanographer, describing his work studying and filming the undersea world.
    ISBN 1-58415-112-9
    1. Cousteau, Jacques Yves—Juvenile literature. 2. Oceanographers—France—Biography—Juvenile literature. [1. Cousteau, Jacques Yves. 2. Oceanographers.] I. Title. II. Series.
GC30.C68 B36 2001
551.46'0092—dc21
[B]   2001038964

ABOUT THE AUTHOR: Born in Boston, Massachusetts, John Bankston began publishing articles in newspapers and magazines while still a teenager. Since then, he has written over two hundred articles, and contributed chapters to books such as *Crimes of Passion* and *Death Row 2000*, which have been sold in bookstores around the world. He has recently written a number of biographies for Mitchell Lane including books on Mandy Moore, Jessica Simpson and Jonas Salk. He currently lives in Los Angeles, California, pursuing a career in the entertainment industry. He has worked as a writer for the movies Dot-Com and the upcoming *Planetary Suicide*, which begins filming in 2002. As an actor John has appeared in episodes of *Sabrina the Teenage Witch*, *Charmed* and *Get Real* along with appearances in the films *Boys and Girls*, and *America So Beautiful*. He has a supporting part in *Planetary Suicide* and has recently completed his first young adult novel, *18 To Look Younger*.

PHOTO CREDITS: cover: Photo Researchers; p. 6 AP Photo; p. 8 Bettmann/Corbis; p. 10 Bettmann/Corbis; p. 16 AP Photo; p. 20 Underwood & Underwood/Corbis; p. 25 AP Photo; p. 28 Bettmann/Corbis; p. 34 Ap Photo/Ah Soon; p. 38 Jean-Michel Productions; p. 39 Photo Researchers; p. 41 Globe Photos; p. 42 AP Photo/Pierre Gleizes; p. 44 AP Photo/Bob Care.

PUBLISHER'S NOTE: In selecting those persons to be profiled in this series, we first attempted to identify the most notable accomplishments of the 20th century in science, medicine, and technology. When we were done, we noted a serious deficiency in the inclusion of women. For the greater part of the 20th century science, medicine, and technology were male-dominated fields. In many cases, the contributions of women went unrecognized. Women have tried for years to be included in these areas, and in many cases, women worked side by side with men who took credit for their ideas and discoveries. Even as we move forward into the 21st century, we find women still sadly underrepresented. It is not an oversight, therefore, that we profiled mostly male achievers. Information simply does not exist to include a fair selection of women.

Contents

Famous oceanographer, inventor, and explorer Jacques Cousteau is pictured in his trademark red cap.

Chapter 1

The Mysteries of the Deep

• •

During the twentieth century, many mysteries that puzzled human beings from the time they first gained the ability to question were solved. In that hundred-year span, modern medicine explained the reasons for infections, examined viruses and described bacteria—which led to the discoveries that provided the cures for tragic diseases that had claimed thousands of victims. Scientists split the atom—dividing nature's smallest known particle into even smaller pieces—at the same time that astronomers proved the universe to be larger than anyone had ever considered.

Space—the final frontier to astronomers and Star Trek fans alike—had many of its riddles explained. The surfaces of the moon, Mars and even distant planets like Neptune and Saturn were revealed.

But despite all of these advances, there still remains a final conquest, a world as misunderstood and complicated as any moon or planet. Less than five percent of its environment has been explored. It is an unknown world within a day's drive for much of the population of the United States.

It is the ocean. While scientists unraveled the mysteries of stars billions of miles away, the dark reaches of the ocean floor just a few miles below the sparkling blue surface remained a question.

The ocean is a part of all of us. It is where life began. The first creatures which slowly escaped from the water and crawled onto land evolved over many millions of years to become human beings. The ocean is so much a part of us that our own life force— our blood—still has a chemical composition very similar to that of sea water.

Yet in many ways the ocean environment is very inhospitable. Explorers must supply their own air. At a few hundred feet the pressure of the water becomes enormous—so great that for many years biologists wrongly assumed no creature could survive it.

Jules Verne was a French author and pioneer of science fiction. He wrote about exploration under the sea long before man was capable of exploring the ocean.

Like space, the ocean was a place that inspired people to describe it in the most fantastic stories. One writer inspired those who dreamed of both places. In the 1860s, Jules Verne's *Twenty Thousand Leagues Under the Sea* described submarines and the kind of diving equipment which would be built over the next century.

But even before Verne's writings, men had begun to take action to uncover its mysteries.

Nearly two hundred years earlier, in the late 1600s, Edmund Halley—the man who discovered the famous comet which bears his name—invented a device to explore this liquid world. The diving bell he crafted had barrels of air attached to its sides and could descend sixty feet with several men safely encased in its shell, protected for up to an hour and a half.

They were just scratching the surface.

In 1837, Augustus Siebe invented a watertight suit attached to a large metal helmet. A long tube connected it to a pump on the surface which supplied air to the diver. It was cumbersome and difficult to manage.

Forty years later, Henry Fleuss developed a self-contained diving device, one which didn't rely on air pumped from the surface but instead allowed the diver to bring his own supply of pure oxygen. Although the oxygen became toxic at a fairly shallow depth, it was the first time a human being was able to move unassisted in the ocean.

And in the twentieth century, another man sought to discover the ocean's secrets. He would shatter diving barriers by going deeper than anyone before him. He developed a system which made it possible for anyone—not just professional divers—to explore the ocean at depths once only imagined. Through filmmaking, he brought the wonders of the ocean into the living rooms of people throughout the world.

As a teenager he was a rowdy youth, a juvenile delinquent even, the kind of kid parents worry about and teachers feel will never amount to anything. He proved them wrong, but not before enduring a tragic accident which first nearly ended his life, and then gave him his life's work. His name is Jacques Cousteau, and this is his story—the story of a man who brought the ocean's mysterious depths to the surface.

Jacques' love of the sea began when he was very young and took swimming lessons. From those humble beginnings, he carved out a career as a famous inventor and explorer. He is shown here in 1986 in front of his famous ship Calypso, which had just been completely overhauled.

Chapter 2

Early Years

● ●

"**J**et set" is a term used to describe people who are usually very well off and spend much of their time flying among places like Paris, London, New York, Palm Beach and similar locations. In many ways, Daniel and Elizabeth Cousteau were members of the "jet set" before jets were even invented.

And they weren't even rich.

Elizabeth and Daniel grew up in Saint-André-de-Cubzac, a quiet coastal community in the Bordeaux region of France. Daniel, the son of a prominent businessman, spent his twenties working as a lawyer and dreaming of adventure before he decided to get married. Elizabeth Duranthon, one of five daughters from the town's richest family, was a pretty 18-year-old when she married 30-year-old Daniel.

Like many young adults who come of age in small towns, the couple dreamed of the excitement and glamour of big city life. For them, the ideal place to live was Paris. At the dawn of the twentieth century, Paris was a city renowned for being a leader in both culture and commerce, a place with well-known nightclubs and international businesses. Just a day's train ride from Saint-André-de-Cubzac, it was a world away from the Cousteaus' provincial hometown.

The couple settled in the city, where Daniel soon located a job as the private secretary and financial adviser for James Hazen Hyde, a young millionaire who traveled for work and pleasure and expected Daniel by his side during his journeys. On most of the trips, Elizabeth traveled as well. When Pierre-Antoine was born, the couple's first child, the birth barely disrupted their globetrotting schedule.

It would take the arrival of the couple's second child to do that.

Elizabeth returned to her home town to give birth. Jacques-Yves Cousteau was born on June 11, 1910, surrounded by relatives. However, despite the family ties, Elizabeth and her newborn returned quickly on a train to Paris. In the beginning the family continued to travel with Hyde—so much so that later, Jacques would describe his earliest memory as waking up on a moving train.

However, while his older brother Pierre seemed to thrive in this fast-paced environment, Jacques was constantly sick, suffering primarily from chronic enteritis—a very painful intestinal inflammation. The illness left the youngster weak and thin.

Although she enjoyed her lifestyle of world travel, Elizabeth eventually began cutting trips short. The long separations between her and her husband added to the family's stress. After a dispute with his employer, Daniel quit and returned home to Paris. For a time, the Cousteaus survived on Elizabeth's family money. In 1918, Daniel was hired by another American millionaire—Eugene Higgins, the man an American newspaper described as "not only the richest, but the handsomest unmarried New Yorker." Higgins' passions ran to fast horses and faster boats. He was also a fitness fanatic, which was unusual in the early 1900s.

Although Elizabeth had curtailed the traveling and placed Jacques in a private school, the boy's health continued to worsen despite the attention of the family doctors. They told the parents that their ailing son should avoid physical activity. When Daniel told his boss about Jacques' ailments, Higgins—who as a rule distrusted the advice that doctors gave anyway—bluntly told the parents that the doctors were completely wrong. Exercise, he told them. Exercise was the key.

And not just any exercise: Jacques should take up swimming. He had learned to swim a few years before, when as a four-year-old he'd spent part of the summer at the French beach resort of Deauville. He'd loved splashing around in the water. Even better was the world below the surface, a world of both serenity and discovery.

As Jacques recalled in *Cousteau*, a biography written by Richard Munson, "When I was four or five years old, I loved touching water. Physically. Sensually. The touch of water fascinated me all the time."

At eight years old, Jacques began swimming as often as he could—in pools, in the Mediterranean, in the ocean—and although his skinny frame meant he was often cold, he got stronger.

So when Higgins brought the Cousteau family with him to New York in 1920, Jacques was well enough to go to summer camp at Harvey's Lake in the scenic and rural state of Vermont. It wasn't just the standard summer camp activities which held the youngster's interest but the chores—one chore in particular.

According to Jacques, his constant clowning angered Mr. Boetz, a German teacher. So Boetz thought he'd punish the boy by making him clear the dead branches and trees from beneath the camp's diving board.

It was hardly punishment.

"I worked very hard," Cousteau recalled in his biography, "diving in that muck without goggles, without a mask, and that's where I learned to dive." He would plunge into the frigid water, each day trying to stay under a little bit longer, fighting the need to breathe.

Since he'd read a book about a man who used a hollowed-out reed to breathe, young Jacques tried it. It didn't work. "The author of my book," he recalled, "like others who wrote diving yarns, had never been on a river bottom with a straw in his mouth."

As Jacques grew older, he developed a variety of interests beyond swimming. He especially loved machines. At age eleven, he used the blueprints for a 200-ton floating crane to construct a four-foot-high electric-powered model. Few machines in the Cousteau household were safe from Jacques' curious fingers as he took apart everything he could.

When he became a teenager, he also became fascinated with another type of machine—the movie camera. With his allowance, he bought a Pathé camera. Through its lens, he could capture the world or even change it. He imagined all number of stories, and film still exists of 16-year-old Jacques playing a villain with a dark suit and painted-on mustache. He even made up his own film company—which he named Société Zix—and always ended his movies with the credits: "producer, director and chief cameraman: J. Cousteau."

Although he was creative with film and gifted with machines, schoolwork was another matter. Jacques hated studying anything he didn't enjoy or think he'd use. His grades were terrible, and his behavior was even worse. He began to get destructive. One day he even smashed out seventeen windows in his school. He was expelled. Although they'd been fairly liberal and permissive in the way they'd raised him, Jacques' parents couldn't take any more. They sent him to a very strict boarding school, one which emphasized discipline above everything.

Although many rambunctious teenagers would have just rebelled more, something about the school's academic structure changed Jacques' behavior. He began focusing more on schoolwork and less on cutting up. "I even studied with a flashlight in bed," he recalled in a later interview.

In 1929, he managed to graduate near the top of his class.

Like many teens, Jacques had no idea what he wanted to do with the rest of his life. There were so many things that interested him that it was hard to settle on a career. He loved making movies—maybe he'd be a film director. Then again, there was his love for the ocean—maybe he'd do something with that.

All he knew was that high school had been hard enough—he didn't want to go to college.

He decided to apply to Ecole Navale, the French naval academy. Like the US Naval Academy in Annapolis, Maryland, the school was very competitive and prestigious. Jacques Cousteau was surprised when he was admitted in 1930, but figured the Navy might give him a chance to try a variety of things and explore the world away from his parents.

Being in the French Navy kept him connected to the ocean. After he graduated in 1933 and became a commissioned officer, his duties aboard ship took him to the Pacific Ocean and Far East for two years, visiting exotic locales like Bali, Japan, and Vietnam. He brought his film equipment everywhere, and crafted a crude documentary of his journeys. The movie even includes footage of an excursion to Hollywood, where he shared a cigarette with movie star Douglas Fairbanks.

When he returned to France in 1935, he was seeking new forms of adventure when he began flight school at Hourtin, a town on the Atlantic Ocean. Even soaring thousands of feet above the earth didn't deter the young filmmaker, who captured footage of staged dogfights—simulated aerial battles—among his classmates.

During a break from flight training that year, the aspiring pilot borrowed his father's Salmson, a luxury sports car, and headed for a wedding. Driving the tiny vehicle was a lot like flying as Cousteau kept pushing it even though night had fallen, taking the treacherous curves through the foothills of the Vosges Mountains with reckless speed.

Along one stretch of the narrow, winding road, the headlights abruptly flickered, then shut off completely. In the sudden darkness, Jacques slammed on the brakes. It was too late.

The convertible flew off the road, flipping several times.

"It was two o'clock in the morning," Jacques Cousteau would later recall, "and I thought I was going to die."

Cousteau's underwater exploration allowed him to go where no men had gone before. In the 1980s, he called Sipadan Island, off the coast of Sabah, east Malaysia, an "untouched piece of art." Just a decade later, this island attracted thousands of divers every year seeking its perfect reefs.

Chapter 3

Il Faut Aller Voir
(We Must Go See for Ourselves)

• •

Waking up in a nearby hospital, Jacques Cousteau was dizzy from agony—both of his arms were badly broken. Through the haze of pain, he tried to listen as a doctor told him some awful news. His right arm was badly infected and would have to be amputated. But even though he was in intense pain, the young man refused to give them permission.

His judgment proved to be correct. He survived the infection and began painful physical therapy. He endured whirlpool baths and exercise. His arm was manipulated by therapists, his fingers twisted and turned. For a long time nothing worked and his arm seemed completely and permanently lifeless.

And then, after eight months of effort, Jacques was able to move his fingers. Just a little. He persisted, increasing his therapy, until he could move his hand.

He'd done it. The arm the doctors had wanted to remove was working again. Unfortunately, despite his progress his right arm would never be as good as it had been and his dreams of becoming a pilot were shattered.

Although this upset Cousteau, he returned to the Navy and began figuring out what other things he could do. Meanwhile, the rest of his classmates continued their flight training and in the years ahead would become combat pilots during World War II. Eventually, all but one of his classmates from flight school died in combat—the accident that had ruined his arm had probably also saved his life.

In his biography, Cousteau says, "It was a test for me. Every morning, every night, I wonder at how lucky I am to still be alive, to have seen so many things and to carry on, being eager to see more."

If the skies no longer beckoned, the ocean was still a possibility. In fact, for Cousteau the attraction was even stronger. In the weightlessness of water, his injury was barely a concern.

In his new assignment for the Navy, Cousteau was assigned to Toulon, a large city on France's Mediterranean coast, as a gunnery instructor. In his new job, Lieutenant Cousteau befriended another young lieutenant, Philippe Tailliez. Like his father's millionaire employer, Tailliez encouraged Cousteau to swim. Although his injury affected his stroke, he began swimming daily and the regular exercise slowly strengthened the limb.

The two lieutenants began spending their free time at Sanary, a tiny beach seven miles from their base. During their ocean explorations, the two met Frédéric Dumas, who told them to call him Didi. Didi loved the ocean so much that he was never far from it, living on a boat or occasionally camping on the sand. He invited the two officers to join him on his boat, exploring the shoreline and fishing.

The three also began diving from the huge rocks which dotted the coast. Like kids on a beach holiday, the men began to compete—seeing how far down they could dive, and who could stay under the longest. Soon they were all reaching depths of thirty feet. Cousteau even reached a point where he could descend past fifty feet.

It was never far enough.

Worse, it seemed like just when he started to see something, he'd have to surface. Just as bad, the salt water made it difficult to keep his eyes open for very long. There were few other places on the planet where man's limits were as obvious as in the ocean.

Cousteau began thinking back to his childhood, when he'd tried to devise a way to breathe during his swims beneath the surface of Harvey's Lake in Vermont. He knew there were ways to survive below the ocean's surface, but most of them involved bulky diving suits with breathing tubes connected to a ship above. The diver was tethered to the surface world and what Cousteau truly wanted was to be able to move around as freely as the fish which darted out of his way when he dove.

The three men brainstormed ideas, coming up with a means to solve the problems of the dives. They began using aviator goggles during their underwater explorations and were able to see clearly. As Cousteau recalled in a 1952 interview with *National Geographic* magazine, "I have been, all my adult life, an officer in the French Navy...Yet I swam and dived as a blind man... Sea goggles opened my eyes upon a new, neglected kingdom. From then on, I never looked back."

As he described it in his biography, it was a world of "wildlife untouched, a jungle at the border of the sea, never seen by those who floated on the opaque roof."

The three men also developed a system of weights so they could descend even deeper. Despite these modest successes, the breathing devices Cousteau invented never worked properly. But he refused to give up.

In the beginning, Cousteau brought a container of pure oxygen down with him. He knew it was dangerous. He didn't care. Despite others' experience, he had to try it for himself.

The first time he descended with the oxygen he deliberately pushed past the 25-foot barrier. Beyond this point, other divers had learned the hard way of oxygen's toxicity. At 40 feet he had a seizure and barely managed to surface.

On his second attempt, he managed to reach 45 feet. He also almost died. "I came very near drowning," he wrote in his journal. "It was the end of my interest in oxygen."

He realized pushing himself this way was dangerous and probably foolhardy. He knew that pure oxygen was different from the air we breathe, which is composed of 78% nitrogen and 21% oxygen with tiny amounts of other gases.

Cousteau realized what he needed to use was compressed air. Unfortunately, when compressed air was released from canisters it escaped too quickly. Divers needed the air to come out slowly, at the same rate they breathe.

For once it wasn't science and experimentation that would help solve Cousteau's dilemma. It was love.

Cousteau had spent his time doing more than just working as a gunnery instructor and diving with his friends. During his long recovery in Paris, he'd met a girl at a party. Her name was Simone Melchior.

A pretty, blonde seventeen-year-old with flashing green eyes and a slim figure, Simone wasn't just pretty but also very smart and funny. Just as important, she shared Cousteau's deep love for the sea because she came from a long line of naval officers.

This is a dive expedition led by Jacques Cousteau to investigate the waters off Abu Dhabi in the Persian Gulf for BP Exploration Company. Here, the dive team is being lowered into the sea in a shark-proof cage.

For a year, she and Cousteau maintained a long distance relationship, though the young man traveled to Paris to see her every chance he got.

Two days before Bastille Day, the anniversary of the date French peasants fought for independence from King Louis XVI, Jacques Cousteau gave up the independence of bachelorhood. On July 12, 1937, he married Simone in a formal wedding, where he wore his uniform and the couple marched beneath the swords of his fellow naval officers.

After their marriage, the two would often dive together, joining his friends Philippe and Didi on their Mediterranean explorations. Simone would continue to dive even after she became pregnant, although eventually she was forced to sit on the shoreline and watch her husband's dives. She gave birth to the couple's first son, Jean-Michel, on May 6, 1938.

Although it would take eight years before he came up with a suit that was completely effective, it was during this year that Cousteau first began developing a diving suit, designed to protect against the cold of the ocean.

Because of his wife, Cousteau was also able to begin developing his own underwater breathing system. It was her father who gave him the guidance he needed. Henri Melchior had followed a distinguished naval career by taking an executive position at Air Liquide. The company manufactured and sold the very gases Jacques needed: oxygen and nitrogen.

Son-in-law and father-in-law sat down and discussed the problem. They realized what they needed was a valve to control the flow of air, a device which was self-regulating. In other words, the diver wouldn't be responsible for controlling the air flow. Just as importantly, the compressed air would regulate air pressure: since water is heavier than air, the pressure inside a diver's lungs must match the pressure of the water on his body.

Jacques Cousteau grew more and more excited as he spoke with his wife's dad. He realized he was close to solving the problem and inventing a device that would allow human beings to swim beneath the water almost as freely as any sea creature.

Unfortunately, evil forces hundreds of miles away would soon threaten the sanctuary of his underwater world.

Adolf Hitler was responsible for plunging the world into World War II. During the war, Jacques Cousteau was a member of an elite underground group of rebel soldiers known as the French Resistance.

Chapter 4
Aqua Lung

● ●

While Cousteau and his wife were enjoying scenic dives with friends, Adolf Hitler was completing plans that would plunge the entire world into the horror of war. The leader of Germany's Nazi party, Hitler had come to power in 1933 and most of his actions after that were intended to increase his nation's power and military might. In September, 1939, the Nazis invaded Poland and quickly subdued it. That was the beginning of World War II.

Less than six months later, German armies poured into France. Unlike the situation in World War I, in which a vast system of trenches extended the war for more than four bloody years, France fell in six weeks. Under the terms of the surrender, Germany was given control of the northern part of France. The southern portion was operated by Marshal Henri Philippe Pétain, a military hero during World War I. It was quickly apparent that Pétain followed the orders of Hitler. Meanwhile, Cousteau's brother Pierre was imprisoned for a time by the Nazis. When he was freed, he was allowed to work for a newspaper in Paris. He often wrote articles against the Jews, who already suffered great persecutions under the Nazi regime.

During this turbulent time, the Cousteau household added a new member when Simone gave birth to another son in December of 1940. The young couple named him Philippe, in honor of Jacques' best friend, Lt. Philippe Tailliez.

Unlike his home country, Jacques Cousteau refused to surrender to the Germans. While he maintained a facade—or false appearance—of working for the French military, in reality he was a member of an elite underground group of rebel soldiers known as the French Resistance. Like those peasants who fought against the royals over one hundred and fifty years before, the men and women of the Resistance risked their lives for their beliefs in freedom.

Under cover of darkness, he spied on the German military and sabotaged their ships. He pretended to be an Italian officer to get information.

Despite his hidden activities, Cousteau was still a member of the French Navy, working as an officer overseeing a gunnery encampment designed to protect Toulon's port. In 1942 he was transferred to Naval Intelligence, and was forced to move to Marseilles, another large city along the shores of the Mediterranean.

While there, he approached his commanding officer with the idea of developing a device to allow a man to breathe underwater. With such a device, he told the commander, a soldier could plant or disable mines, and approach the enemy unseen from beneath the water.

The commander agreed, and helped Cousteau get a permit from the International Committee for the Exploration of the Mediterranean. He would later recall that he was often stopped by Nazis but the card allowed him to go where he wished. Besides, most of them considered him a harmless guy with a weird fascination for the sea. He never did anything to convince them otherwise.

Although Cousteau didn't know it then, he wasn't alone in trying to develop an underwater breathing device for the military. He'd later learn the Nazis had been working feverishly to develop their own system.

In the beginning, there was little success. Cousteau began his underwater experiments using a device known as the Fernez pump, which connected a breathing hose from the diver to the ship hovering above him. Jacques hated it and complained he felt like he was on a leash. He wanted to be free. During one dive using the Fernez pump, the hose detached while he was forty feet below. He almost drowned.

It was the last time he used the device.

Everything changed when Cousteau met the man who'd made it possible for the French to substitute cooking oil for gasoline, which was both rare and expensive during the war. Lt. Cousteau was introduced to Emile Gagnan by his father-in-law. Gagnan had created a valve that would allow the French to use cooking oil rather than gasoline—most of which was taken over by the German army for their vehicles—in their cars. Cousteau was especially interested because the device was self-regulating.

Jacques and wife, Simone, aboard the Calypso, on August 30, 1959, in New York Harbor.

At first Cousteau thought he had his breakthrough. Over a few short weeks he and Gagnan developed an underwater breathing device that consisted of a large metal container of compressed air which was connected to a mouthpiece by a tube. All of it was regulated by Gagnan's invention.

Nervous about the Nazis discovering their work, the two men abandoned the Mediterranean and instead tested their device on an isolated stretch of the Marne River. At first, as he swam beneath the water's surface, Cousteau was confident that the device was the discovery he'd dreamed of. Until he stood up. Or moved in any way other than straight ahead. Then the air became unregulated. The tank was useless.

Gasping, Jacques surfaced and according to his biography, yelled, "The darn thing runs wide open when you are standing and it gets hard to breathe when you are upside down!"

The first test was a failure. The two began shouting at each other on the way back to Paris. The argument actually helped; by the time they arrived at Gagnan's laboratory, they had a solution. The device they'd tested had placed the exhaust six inches higher than the air intake. Turning it upside down blocked the air flow.

It only took a minor adjustment before they finally had a tank that would offer air to an underwater diver regardless of the direction the tank was pointed in. Consisting of metal cylinders that together weighed fifty pounds and a fist-sized regulator, the device was crude. But when they tried out the device in a large tank of water, it worked.

In June of 1943, Cousteau gave it a much more realistic test, in the Mediterranean Sea off the French Riviera. His buddy Didi stayed ashore, ready to rescue him if something went wrong.

In the water's weightlessness, the heft of the compressed air tanks didn't matter. "I experimented with all possible maneuvers—loops, somersaults, and barrel rolls," Cousteau wrote in his journal. "I stood upside down on one finger and burst out laughing, a shrill distorted laugh. Nothing I did altered the automatic rhythm of the air. Delivered from gravity and buoyancy I flew around in space."

Afterwards, Cousteau removed a few lobsters from a cave, and along with Simone, Didi and several friends, enjoyed a seafood feast celebrating the successful test.

Gagnan and Cousteau had invented the first self-contained underwater breathing apparatus, or SCUBA, the name it would eventually acquire. They took out a patent, meaning no one else would be able to claim the invention. They called it the "Aqua Lung" and it would forever change the way people were able to explore the ocean depths. And for Cousteau, who had explored the limits of safe diving when all he had was a lungful of air, the Aqua Lung would allow him to go further than he'd ever thought possible.

Jacques demonstrates his latest invention, the Aqua-Lung. The Aqua-Lung allowed divers to breathe at depths up to 200 feet without any above water connections. (1950)

At one point in his long career, Jacques searched the undersea world for the legendary city of Atlantis.

Chapter 5

Rapture of the Deep

● ●

Venturing into the unknown is always risky. Scientists have given their lives testing vaccines; astronauts have died in flight tests and on launch pads; explorers in uncharted territories have vanished with no trace. The Aqua Lung would exact its own grim toll.

With the new device, the three friends—Jacques Cousteau, Philippe Tailliez and Didi Dumas—began hundreds of tests during the summer of 1943. They dove beyond one hundred feet, where sunlight was barely present and the water was murky. Many scientists believed any plant or animal life at that depth would be equally colorless. Cousteau would prove them wrong by showing them the evidence.

Once during his tests with the Aqua Lung, he speared a fish far below the water's surface. At that depth, he noticed the creature's blood was a brilliant green and only became bright red when it reached the surface. He realized then that the world of the deep ocean was one of incredible color.

Cousteau decided he wanted to show the surface world his discovery. His childhood passion for making movies suddenly came in handy.

No one had made an underwater movie before. Besides the difficulty of maneuvering prior to the aqua lung, there just weren't any movie cameras designed to be used underwater. Because both the film and the moving parts within the camera would be useless if they got wet, the device needed to be waterproof.

Since there wasn't an underwater motion picture camera available, Cousteau decided to build his own. He bought an old camera for twenty-five dollars and built a case around it.

But his now-waterproof camera had another problem: There was no way to adjust the focus of the lens. The images would come out fuzzy, making them basically useless. So

Cousteau turned a clothes pin into a lever and secured it to the focus pull.

Now he had to overcome a third problem. During wartime, movie film was as hard to come by as gasoline. Besides, as a naval officer he had no official need for it. If he requested some, that might arouse the suspicions of the Gestapo, the dreaded German secret police.

Again Cousteau's ingenuity came to the rescue. He bought rolls of regular still camera film and, huddling underneath his blankets so that no light could enter and prematurely expose the film, taped it into fifty-foot strips. He and his friends also used a studio light connected to their boat's generator, which enabled them to illuminate the murky world below.

He was ready to make a movie.

The first film he produced was called *18 Meters Down*. When it premiered at the Cannes Film Festival several years later, it would give the audience their first glimpse of the planet's undersea world.

It is a happy adult who is able to do just some of the things he dreamed of as a child. Cousteau was very lucky, because he was able to do nearly everything. He was able to utilize his teenage love of taking apart machines and apply it to the new inventions his career required. He used these skills every day in order to create new movie cameras and other equipment, not to mention keeping them running despite the damaging effects of salt water. He was able to use his motion picture skills to create movies which in his lifetime would reach a global audience and make him as well known as any Hollywood filmmaker.

Best of all, his daily life connected him to the water, to an environment he'd fallen in love with as a kid.

Despite these opportunities, the grim reality of World War II meant Cousteau had to think about life beyond the sea. Besides his interest in marine life, he was constantly imagining ways the Aqua Lung could be used against the Nazis.

In November, 1944, Cousteau traveled to London to persuade the Allies—primarily the United States and England—to use his Aqua Lung in the final push against the Germans. But despite his best efforts, the military leaders he met with in London refused to consider the Aqua Lung. They believed the invention had arrived too late in the war effort to make a difference. Then again, perhaps he was just ahead of his time. Today elite fighting forces such as the Navy SEALS employ breathing gear similar to Cousteau's Aqua Lung in a variety of military operations.

In one respect the men in London were correct—the war was almost over. Germany surrendered the following May. For his heroic efforts with the French Resistance, Jacques Cousteau was awarded the Legion d'Honneur, France's highest military award.

Although he was briefly assigned a desk job and his friend Tailliez was given the unlikely position of forest ranger, Cousteau managed to quickly convince the military that the two men's skills were being wasted. They were soon transferred back to the base at Toulon, where they formed the Undersea Research Group. They even hired Didi Dumas as an equipment specialist.

Eventually the Undersea Research Group had trucks, motorcycles, and three vessels including a large diving boat, the *Albatross*, which could handle ocean explorations. Three petty officers were assigned to the new unit: Maurice Fargues, Jean Pinard and Guy Morandière. Didi trained the trio until all were proficient in diving.

Following the war, the harbors and waters surrounding coastal France were dotted with mines, explosive devices designed to go off on contact. The first mission of the Undersea Research Group was to locate and disarm these devices. It was very dangerous work. Aboard one sunken ship, Cousteau began examining a group of cylinders he didn't recognize. He was busy scraping algae from one of them when Didi fiercely pulled on his arm, yanking him out of the ship and to the surface. Sputtering, Cousteau asked Didi what was going on—and quickly learned that he'd been toying with one of the most dangerous mines the Germans had ever invented, one which could be set off by the slightest noise or motion!

This time, the men realized there was nothing they could do. They roped off the surrounding area and waited for the corrosive effects of saltwater to take their toll on the triggering mechanisms.

Besides his work with the mines, Cousteau continued to make films, including one sponsored by the French Navy entitled *A Dive of the Rubris*. The short movie captured the French submarine *Rubris* as it launched an unarmed torpedo past the camera, again showing movie audiences something they'd never seen before.

For the men of the Undersea Research Group, the biggest danger lay not from mines but from the water itself. Because diving with just an aqua lung was new, no one was sure at what depth it would become dangerous. Finding out would cost one man his life.

"Rapture of the deep" is the name given to the body's reaction when nitrogen builds up in the blood. On land, people breathe nitrogen in and out all the time. However, when divers descend below a certain depth, this gas begins to accumulate in their bloodstream.

This accumulation of nitrogen begins to affect the nervous system. The victim begins to feel drugged and often takes stupid risks. Some divers have been known to remove their mouthpiece and offer air to a passing fish.

In 1947, Jacques and his men embarked on a series of tests designed to establish the limits of safe diving. First they dropped a shot line—or weighted rope—overboard. The shot line had boards attached every few feet, and when a diver dove as far as he felt comfortable he would sign his name on the depth board before returning to the surface.

In order to prevent any problems, each diver had a safety rope tied to his waist and anchored to the boat. If anything went wrong, the diver was supposed to tug on the rope and he would be pulled up. As an extra precaution, another diver was suited up with an aqua lung and prepared to go under water immediately if anything went wrong.

As summer turned to fall, Jacques held the record: 297 feet. "We went lower," he would later write, "because that was the only way to learn more about the drunken effect, and to sample individual reaction on what aqualung work could be done in severe depths."

Besides just wanting to prove some scientific theory, there was still an intensely competitive spirit among the men. They all wanted to beat Cousteau's record.

Maurice Fargues, one of the new guys, had joined shortly after the Undersea Research Group was formed. He was in the best physical shape of all the men. He was sure he could break the record.

He sent back constant tugs on the rope after he dove, letting everyone on the surface know he was okay. Jean Pinard, the safety man, waited nervously.

And then the signal stopped.

The rope stopped moving.

Pinard immediately plunged below. In moments he reached the 150 foot depth. Fargues was hanging loosely, like a man at the end of a noose. His mouthpiece was disconnected.

Pinard and the rest of the crew raced to pull Fargues to the surface; very quickly his body was on the boat's deck. They spent twelve hours trying to revive him but their efforts were futile.

Maurice Fargues was dead.

The man had given his life to scrawl his name on the board marking 396 feet. "Fargues gave his life a hundred feet below our greatest penetrations," Cousteau would write.

After that, Jacques Cousteau set the limit at 300 feet. Anything greater could be fatal. Besides, there were other boundaries to explore.

Cables lift the Calypso at a Singapore shipyard on January 25, 1996. The shipped tipped over and sank on January 8 after being hit by a barge on Singapore's west coast.

Chapter 6

Calypso

• •

In the 1930s, William Beebe and Otis Barton developed a spherical, watertight diving saucer called a bathysphere, from the Greek words "bathy" for deep and "sphere" for ball. Paid for by the New York Zoological Society and the National Geographic Society, it had its own self-contained breathing system and could reach a depth of 3,028 feet.

In 1948, Auguste Piccard, who'd once set a world record by going up eleven miles in a balloon, decided to test the limits of the ocean. He developed his own version of the bathysphere, a device he called a bathyscaph, or "deep boat."

He promised to descend five times deeper than any man before him, using the device which had its own oxygen generator along with movie cameras and lighting equipment.

Jacques Cousteau was immediately interested. His wife, Simone, wasn't. "No one ordered you to go," his biography records her saying. "Don't risk yourself in that craziness."

Despite his wife's pleas, Cousteau couldn't resist getting an invitation to accompany Auguste on his maiden voyage. Although he never dove with the bathyscaph, Jacques watched as the Swiss professor fought to overcome a series of mechanical problems which delayed the launch by five days. When he finally did get the device to work, he reached a depth of 4,600 feet, which was far less than he'd promised. It would take his third vessel, the FNRSIII, to gain a world record with its 12,500-foot descent.

Despite the problems Piccard had encountered, Cousteau realized he too wanted to have his own crew, his own ship. Friends joked the only way he'd get his own ship was to become an admiral in the French Navy. Considering that he'd only risen to the rank of captain—the lowest ranking officer among his graduating class at the Naval Academy—this wasn't very likely.

What Jacques Cousteau needed was someone who both believed in his dream and had the means to pay for it.

Digging through his address book, Cousteau came across the name of a man he'd met at a party earlier. Loël Guinness was a wealthy man who enjoyed supporting causes he believed in. Cousteau quickly convinced the man not only to fund the purchase of a ship, but also to pay for the work necessary to turn it into a first class vessel of ocean exploration.

After talking the Navy into giving him a three-month leave of absence, Cousteau went out looking for his ship. He had a good idea of what he wanted: a surplus minesweeper from World War II. Minesweepers were built especially solidly because they were expected not only to locate mines but also detonate them. The hull had to be able to withstand the shock waves from the nearby explosions. In addition, they were very easy to handle and didn't draw much water, so they could work close to shore or among coral reefs.

Cousteau made a trip to Malta, an island in the middle of the Mediterranean, and found what would eventually become one of the most famous vessels in the world. Her name was *Calypso*, she was 150 feet long, weighed 360 tons and was built in 1942.

In Greek mythology, Calypso was a sea nymph who sheltered the weary hero Odysseus as he struggled home following the Trojan War. It was a perfect name for a ship that would shelter scientists and divers as they struggled to unlock the secrets of the undersea world.

Unfortunately, Guinness' donation wasn't enough to pay for everything Cousteau needed. He wound up using some of his own money to buy modern research equipment. His father-in-law helped him get donations and Simone even sold some of her jewelry. The money paid for enlarged crew quarters, a high observation platform over the ship's bridge and a chamber eight feet below the water line. The work on the ship took nearly a year; as always, Cousteau's friends Philippe Tailliez and Didi Dumas contributed ideas.

Sadly, while Cousteau was working on the ship, his mother died from a stroke. She'd been visiting his brother Pierre, who was in prison for his involvement with the Nazis during the war.

On November 24, 1951, the ship left the waters of the Mediterranean for the Red Sea. Simone joined her husband on the ship's maiden voyage.

In many ways, life aboard the Calypso was like life aboard no other ship. Cousteau, wearing the red cap he became known for, was obviously in charge. Still, everyone on board the ship pitched in—helping to do the dishes, fix the meals, clean the deck. Simone ran the sonar, a device used to measure the depth of the ocean floor. Even their children helped out, joining the diving teams and taking on a variety of jobs as young teenagers.

Since Cousteau lacked formal training in marine biology, he hired a variety of scientists, men with "Dr." before their names. But on board *Calypso*, doctors were called "mister" and those without degrees were called "doctor."

Except for Jacques. He would remain known as "Captain Cousteau" even after he left the French Navy several years later.

While his earlier films gained him respect, it was his work with *Calypso* that would make him rich and famous.

In 1952, Cousteau traveled to the United States and met with the leaders of the National Geographic Society. The organization, which had been funding explorers for decades, agreed to finance his explorations. Among the expeditions he filmed for the organization was his discovery of an ancient shipwreck. The vessel, believed to have sunk over 2,000 years before, yielded a variety of finds, including a number of unopened bottles of wine. During his work there, Cousteau developed a special movie camera designed to capture his work inside the ship. He also sampled some of the vintage wine.

While his work with the National Geographic Society went a long way toward helping pay for his dreams, it would take a book to make him famous.

Written with his friend Didi Dumas, *The Silent World* was a best seller in 1953 with over half a million copies sold. By the end of the year, it would be rare for Cousteau and his crew to land anywhere without being asked for their autographs. The next year, he teamed up with young French filmmaker Louis Malle to produce a film version of the book. The final result would win the top prize at the famous Cannes Film Festival and the Academy Award for Best Documentary.

Jacques' son, Jean-Michel, followed closely in his father's footsteps. He, too, is an oceanographer, explorer, filmmaker, and marine conservationist. Here he is shown observing three bannerfish as he dives along a coral reef called Nuggets in Savusavu Bay near Fiji.

As Cousteau's work steadily gained a larger audience, the opportunities for *Calypso* continued to increase.

In the early 1960s, Jacques Cousteau appeared on the cover of *Time* magazine. He was awarded National Geographic's Gold Medal by President John F. Kennedy in a White House ceremony. He won a second Academy Award in 1964 for his documentary, *World Without Sun.*

The film depicted life inside the Conshelf II, an experimental underwater living station. Cousteau developed several of these structures, which were placed on the Continental Shelf, the underwater portion of a continent extending several miles past the shoreline.

Although these structures—including Starfish House and Conshelfs I, II, and III—provided valuable data about the ocean and the effects of living in such an environment, they were also very expensive and plagued by mechanical problems.

For Cousteau, the best opportunities still lay with his film work. In April of 1966, he signed a deal with ABC television for a series of one-hour specials over the course of eight years. The network would pay Jacques over four million dollars!

Between the years of 1968 to 1976, the television series "The Undersea World of Jacques Cousteau" introduced countless millions of viewers to *Calypso*, Cousteau and the other divers. He narrated each film and his gentle voice became as familiar as that of network newscasters.

The entire deal had been negotiated by Cousteau's son, Philippe, who had taken over many of the business arrangements involving *Calypso*. His work required him to travel from his home in Los Angeles to New York and wherever the *Calypso* was. Jacques' other son, Jean-Michel, worked in filmmaking and was also very involved in his dad's work.

But while Cousteau's career as an ocean explorer was improving every year, his family life went through some unhappy changes.

Jacques Cousteau was elected director of the Oceanographic Museum in Monaco by the governing board. This is a photo of the museum called "The Rock."

On June 25, 1997, Jacques Cousteau died in Paris, France. His funeral was attended by thousands from around the world.

Chapter 7
A Time of Sadness

For Jacques Cousteau the ocean world he'd embraced as a child had provided a lifetime of serenity. Unfortunately, life above the water was not so calm. Both of his sons were very valuable to him—Philippe as a businessman and Jean-Michel as a diver and cameraman. The work of the *Calypso* was in many ways a family business.

For Philippe the rift with his father wasn't because of work but because of love. In the late 1960s, during his work for the *Calypso*, Philippe met an American model named Janice Sullivan. When he became engaged to the twenty-six-year-old, his parents were furious. They couldn't believe he wasn't going to marry a French woman. They showed their displeasure by refusing to attend the couple's wedding in 1967. For a gift, the Cousteaus sent their son's bride a French language course.

Although Philippe continued to work for his father, his parents' attitude toward Janice affected his relationship with them. Jean-Michel and he began to compete to handle their father's business affairs. While father and son eventually made up, there would always be some friction between the two.

In 1979, Philippe was killed in a plane crash on board *The Flying Calypso*, a seaplane. Jacques Cousteau was torn apart by his son's death. In a later interview, Jean-Michel remembered his father saying, "I need you. I must have your help or else I will quit."

Jean-Michael replied, "I told him, 'I'm in, don't say another word. It's taken care of.'"

Despite the loss, Cousteau continued his ocean exploration work.

In 1973, six years before Philippe's death, Cousteau had started the non-profit Cousteau Society to raise money for ocean exploration and research as well as protecting ocean life. It currently numbers more than 300,000 members all over the world

Jacques poses in front of a giant blue whale on the Champs-Elysee in June 1989 for the promotion of his marine museum in Paris.

and has taken a leading role in making people aware of the dangers to the oceanic environment.

For his efforts and many contributions to marine science, Cousteau received the Medal of Freedom from US President Ronald Reagan in 1985. Four years later, his native France honored him by making a member of the French Academy.

But in 1990, Simone died of cancer. On January 11, 1996, Cousteau's beloved *Calypso*—which had become famous to millions of television viewers—sank in the harbor of Singapore.

Jacques Cousteau died in his Paris apartment on June 25, 1997. By that time, he'd revealed the ocean world to untold millions of people, including more than ten million divers in the United States alone. Beyond what he'd done with his filmmaking and his inventions, he'd also been a leader in environmental causes, one of the first to speak out about the effects of pollution on the ocean.

"There is no death possible in the oceans," he said in his online interview with *The Environmental Magazine*. "There will always be life—but they're getting sicker every year...We have to prepare for what life could become in forty years."

This whale skeleton was reassembled on the beach in Antarctica by Jacques Cousteau.

Divers pretend to play musical instruments at the Underwater Music Festival at the Looe Key National Marine Sanctuary in the Florida Keys on July 12, 1997. The "concert" was a partial tribute to oceanographer, Jacques Cousteau.

Jacques Cousteau Chronology

- 1910, born to Daniel and Elizabeth Cousteau in Saint-André-de-Cubzac, France
- 1918, begins swimming for health
- 1920, attends summer camp at Harvey's Lake in Vermont
- 1926, attends very strict boarding school in Ribeauville, France
- 1929, graduates from high school
- 1930, attends French naval academy at Brest
- 1933, finishes naval officer training and travels throughout Asia
- 1935, begins pilot training
- 1936, badly injured while driving father's sports car
- 1937, marries Simone Melchior
- 1938, birth of son Jean-Michel Cousteau
- 1940, birth of son Philippe Cousteau
- 1943, designs the Aqua Lung in collaboration with Emile Gagnan
- 1943, produces his first professional film
- 1945, forms underseas research group
- 1951, begins maiden voyage with *Calypso*, his research vessel
- 1955, begins filming *The Silent World* with French director Louis Malle
- 1956, wins top award at Cannes Film Festival
- 1957, wins Academy Award for Best Documentary
- 1964, wins Academy Award for film about Conshelf II
- 1973, founds the Cousteau Society
- 1990, Simone Melchior Cousteau dies
- 1997, dies of respiratory disease

Timeline of Invention

- **5000 BC**, Suzerain civilization creates story of Gilgamesh, a king who breathes underwater through a seaweed tube
- **900 BC**, Assyrian artwork depicts underwater breathing device
- **1400s**, Florentine artist and engineer Leonardo da Vinci draws pictures of diving machines
- **1690**, Edmund Halley invents the diving bell

- **1700s**, American statesman and scientist Benjamin Franklin crafts fins for swimmers to wear
- **1790s**, Robert Fulton develops submarine for Napoleon Bonaparte
- **1837**, Augustus Siebe invents watertight diving suit with a large helmet attached to the body and an air pump to the surface which supplies air to the diver.
- **1844**, Henri Milne Edwards' explorations of ocean life using a device similar to Siebe's provide first accounts of life in ocean.
- **1855**, Matthew Fountain Maury publishes first oceanography textbook, *The Physical Geography of the Sea*
- **1865**, French Naval Lt. Augustus Denayrouse and mining engineer Benoit Rouquayrol develop tank connected to air on surface which allows dives up to 165 feet
- **1876**, Henry Fleuss develops first self-contained diving apparatus using compressed oxygen
- **1878**, Frenchman Paul Bert conducts experiments on divers' reactions to nitrogen
- **1892**, Louis Bouton makes the first underwater photographs
- **1911**, Sir Robert Davis improves Fleuss's design and develops tank used by military "frogmen" because it doesn't emit bubbles
- **1926**, Yves Le Prieur develops first high-pressure cylinder to use ordinary air, but it isn't self-regulating
- **1930**, William Beebe descends 1,426 feet in his bathyscape
- **1943**, Cousteau and Emile Gagnan redesign Gagnan's cooking oil valve to regulate air flow and invent the first SCUBA tank—the aqua lung

For Further Reading

Young adults

DuTemple, Lesley A. *A&E Biography: Jacques Cousteau*. Minneapolis, MN: Lerner Publications, 2000.

Reef, Catherine. *Jacques Cousteau: Champion of the Sea*. Frederick, MD: Twenty First Century Books, 1992

Adult

Munson, Richard. *Cousteau: The Captain and His World*. New York: William Morrow and Company, 1989.

Prager, Ellen. *The Oceans*. New York: McGraw-Hill, 2000.

Books by Jacques Cousteau

The Ocean World. New York: Abradale Press/Harry Abrams, 1979. 1993 edition published by Harry Abrams (Times Mirror).

The Silent World, with Frédéric Dumas. Oxford: Clio Press, 1953.

On the Web:

www.cousteau.org

www.dolphinlog.org

www.incwell.com/Biographies/Cousteau.html

Glossary

amputation - cutting off a limb

aqua lung - tank containing compressed air which regulates air pressure so divers can breathe under water.

continental shelf - edge of the continent which extends several miles past the shoreline

environment - the physical world that surrounds a plant or animal

minesweeper - wooden-hulled boat used during World War Two to find mines and explode them

nitrogen - inert gas composing more than 75% of the air we breathe

nitrogen narcosis - "rapture of the deep," a drugged feeling encountered by divers descending too far caused by nitrogen gas building up in their bloodstream

oxygen - colorless, odorless gas necessary for our survival that makes up about 20% of the earth's atmosphere

regulator - device on an aqua lung that admits the right amount of compressed air to a diver's lungs

SCUBA - Self Contained Underwater Breathing Apparatus (see aqua lung)

water pressure - the weight of water which causes pressure on the body

Index